HUMAN RIGHTS
AND
PRISONS

Human Rights

A Pocketbook of
International Human Rights
Standards for Prison Officials

Professional
Training
Series No.
11 Add. 3

UNITED NATIONS

UNITED NATIONS
New York and Geneva, 2005

NOTE

The designations employed and the presentation of the material in this publication do not imply the expression of any opinion whatsoever on the part of the Secretariat of the United Nations concerning the legal status of any country, territory, city or area, or of its authorities, or concerning the delimitation of its frontiers or boundaries.

Material contained in this publication may be freely quoted or reprinted, provided credit is given and a copy of the publication containing the reprinted material is sent to the Office of the United Nations High Commissioner for Human Rights, Palais des Nations, 8-14 avenue de la Paix, CH-1211 Geneva 10, Switzerland.

———— ▓ ————

UN2

ST/HR/P/PT/11/Add.3

HR/P/PT/11/Add.3

UNITED NATIONS PUBLICATION
Sales No. E.04.XIV.5
ISBN 92-1-154158-1
ISSN 1020-1688

NOTE TO USERS OF THE POCKETBOOK

This Pocketbook is one component of the four-part publication *Human Rights and Prisons* – a human rights training package for prison officials. The four components are designed to complement each other and, taken together, provide all necessary elements for the conduct of human rights training programmes for prison officials, under the training approach developed by the Office of the United Nations High Commissioner for Human Rights.

The **Manual** (component one of the package) provides in-depth information on sources, systems and standards for human rights relating to the work of prison officials, practical recommendations, topics for discussion, case studies and checklists.

The **Compilation** (component two of the package) includes excerpts from and full texts of selected international human rights instruments concerning the administration of justice.

The **Trainer's Guide** (component three of the package) provides instructions and tips for trainers to be used together with the Manual in conducting training courses for prison officials.

This **Pocketbook** of international human rights standards (component four of the package) is designed to be a readily accessible and portable reference for prison officials, containing a comprehensive collection of point-form standards organized according to prison officials' duties and functions, and topics, and referenced with detailed footnotes.

Copies of the Manual, the Compilation, the Trainer's Guide and this Pocketbook may be obtained from:

Office of the United Nations High Commissioner for Human Rights
Palais des Nations
8-14 avenue de la Paix
CH-1211 Geneva 10 Switzerland

web site: *www.ohchr.org*
e-mail: *publications@ohchr.org*

CONTENTS

ABBREVIATIONS FOR INTERNATIONAL INSTRUMENTS CITED IN THE POCKETBOOK

Beijing Rules	United Nations Standard Minimum Rules for the Administration of Juvenile Justice (The Beijing Rules)
BPT	Basic Principles for the Treatment of Prisoners
CAT	Convention against Torture and Other Cruel, Inhuman or Degrading Treatment or Punishment
CEDAW	Convention on the Elimination of All Forms of Discrimination against Women
Code of Conduct	Code of Conduct for Law Enforcement Officials
CRC	Convention on the Rights of the Child
Death Penalty Safeguards	Safeguards guaranteeing protection of the rights of those facing the death penalty
Declaration on Enforced Disappearance	Declaration on the Protection of All Persons from Enforced Disappearance
Declaration on Violence against Women	Declaration on the Elimination of Violence against Women
ICCPR	International Covenant on Civil and Political Rights

ICESCR	International Covenant on Economic, Social and Cultural Rights
Principles of Medical Ethics	Principles of Medical Ethics relevant to the Role of Health Personnel, particularly Physicians, in the Protection of Prisoners and Detainees against Torture and Other Cruel, Inhuman or Degrading Treatment or Punishment
Principles on Detention or Imprisonment	Body of Principles for the Protection of All Persons under Any Form of Detention or Imprisonment
Principles on Force and Firearms	Basic Principles on the Use of Force and Firearms by Law Enforcement Officials
Principles on Summary Executions	Principles on the Effective Prevention and Investigations of Extra-legal, Arbitrary and Summary Executions
Robben Island Guidelines	Guidelines and Measures for Prohibition and Prevention of Torture, Cruel, Inhuman or Degrading Treatment or Punishment in Africa (The Robben Island Guidelines)
Rules for Juveniles	United Nations Rules for the Protection of Juveniles Deprived of their Liberty

SMR	Standard Minimum Rules for the Treatment of Prisoners
Tokyo Rules	United Nations Standard Minimum Rules for Non-custodial Measures (The Tokyo Rules)
UDHR	Universal Declaration of Human Rights

INTERNATIONAL HUMAN RIGHTS
STANDARDS FOR PRISON OFFICIALS*

I.   General Principles

International human rights law is binding on all States and their agents, including prison officials.[1]

Human rights are a legitimate subject for international law and international scrutiny.[2]

Law enforcement officials are obliged to know, and to apply, international standards for human rights.[3]

II.   Right to Physical and Moral IntegritySTART

All human beings are born free and equal in dignity and rights.[4]

---

* For the precise language of the provisions as contained in the international instruments, those instruments should be consulted directly. Almost all the instruments cited are reproduced in component two of this training package, Human Rights and Prisons: A Compilation of International *Human Rights Instruments concerning the Administration of Justice* (Office of the United Nations High Commissioner for Human Rights (OHCHR), Professional Training Series No. 9/Add.1); and OHCHR, *Human Rights: A Compilation of International Instruments*, vol. I (2 parts), Universal Instruments (United Nations publication, Sales No. E.02.XIV.4).

Human rights derive from the inherent dignity of the human person.[5]

All persons deprived of their liberty shall be treated at all times with humanity and with respect for the inherent dignity of the human person.[6]

No one shall be subjected to torture or to cruel, inhuman or degrading treatment or punishment. There are no exceptions.[7]

Torture is defined as any act by which severe physical or mental pain or suffering is intentionally inflicted on a person, other than that which is inherent in or incidental to lawful sanctions.[8]

Ill-treatment is defined as other acts of cruel, inhuman or degrading treatment or punishment which do not amount to torture.[9]

Any act of torture committed as part of a widespread or systematic attack directed against any civilian population, with knowledge of the attack, is a crime against humanity.[10]

No prisoner shall be subjected, even with his or her consent, to any medical or scientific experimentation which may be detrimental to health.[11]

Like torture and ill-treatment, enforced disappearances and summary executions are completely prohibited.[12]

All law enforcement officials shall be fully informed and educated about the prohibition of torture and ill-treatment.[13]

Any statement made as a result of torture shall not be invoked as evidence in any proceedings, except as evidence to bring the perpetrators to justice.[14]

Orders from a superior officer may not be invoked as a justification of torture.[15]

Law enforcement officials may use force only when it is strictly necessary.[16]

Any individual who alleges that he or she has been subjected to torture has the right to complain and to have the case promptly and impartially examined by competent authorities.[17]

All deaths in custody and disappearances of prisoners shall be properly investigated.[18]

All interrogation rules, instructions, methods and practices pertaining to detained and imprisoned persons shall be kept under systematic review with a view to preventing torture.[19]

Persons deprived of their liberty shall be held in places which are officially recognized as places of custody.[20]

A detailed register shall be kept of every person deprived of liberty.[21]

All prisoners shall be provided promptly with written information about the regulations which apply to them and on their rights and obligations.[22]

The families, legal representatives and, if appropriate, diplomatic missions of prisoners are to receive full information about the fact of their detention and where they are held.[23]

All prisoners shall be offered a proper medical examination and treatment as soon as possible after admission.[24]

III. Right to an Adequate Standard of Living

All persons deprived of their liberty shall be treated with humanity and with respect for the inherent dignity of the human person.[25]

All persons deprived of their liberty shall have the right to an adequate standard of living, including adequate food, drinking water, accommodation, clothing and bedding.[26]

Accommodation for prisoners shall provide adequate cubic content of air, floor space, lighting, heating and ventilation.[27]

Prisoners required to share sleeping accommodation shall be carefully selected and supervised at night.[28]

Adequate food and drinking water are human rights.[29]

All prisoners shall be provided with wholesome and adequate food at the usual hours and with drinking water available whenever needed.[30]

Clothing as a component of the right to an adequate standard of living is a human right.[31]

All prisoners not allowed to wear their own clothing shall be provided with suitable clothing.[32]

There shall be facilities for keeping clothing clean and in proper condition.[33]

All prisoners shall be provided with a separate bed and clean bedding, with facilities for keeping bedding clean.[34]

There must be facilities to wash and dry clothing and bedding regularly.[35]

IV. Health Rights of Prisoners

The enjoyment of the highest attainable standard of physical and mental health is a human right.[36]

It is a basic requirement that all prisoners should be given a medical examination as soon as they have been admitted to a prison or place of detention.[37]

Any necessary medical treatment should then be provided free of charge.[38]

Prisoners should generally have the right to request a second medical opinion.[39]

Prisoners and all detained persons have the right to the highest attainable standard of physical and mental health.[40]

Prisoners should have free access to the health services available in the country.[41]

Decisions about a prisoner's health should be taken only on medical grounds by medically qualified people.[42]

The medical officer has an important responsibility to ensure that proper health standards are met. He or she can do this by regularly inspecting and advising the director of the prison on the suitability of food, water, hygiene, cleanliness, sanitation, heating, lighting, ventilation, clothing, bedding and opportunities for exercise.[43]

Every prison should have proper health facilities and medical staff to provide for a range of health needs, including dental and psychiatric care. Sick prisoners who cannot be treated in the prison, such as prisoners with mental illness, should be transferred to a civilian hospital or to a specialized prison hospital.[44]

All prisoners shall have access to a qualified dental practitioner.[45]

Services for psychiatric diagnosis and, if appropriate, treatment shall be available at every prison.[46]

Prisoners who are insane shall not be detained in prisons, but transferred as soon as possible to mental institutions.[47]

Prisoners suffering from other mental diseases shall be treated in specialized institutions under medical management.[48]

During their stay in a prison, insane and mentally ill prisoners shall be supervised by a medical officer.[49]

It is important that health care for prisoners be provided by at least one qualified medical officer.[50]

Medical personnel have a duty to provide prisoners and detainees with health care equal to that which is afforded to those who are not imprisoned or detained.[51]

The primary responsibility of health-care personnel is to protect the health of all prisoners.[52]

Health-care personnel shall not commit or give their permission for any acts which may adversely affect the health of prisoners.[53]

All prisoners shall be provided with facilities to meet the needs of nature in a clean and decent manner and to maintain adequately their own cleanliness and good appearance.[54]

No prisoner shall be punished before being informed of the alleged offence and having the opportunity to present a proper defence.[63]

No prisoner shall be employed in any disciplinary capacity.[64]

All cruel, inhuman or degrading punishments are completely prohibited, including corporal punishment or placing in a dark cell.[65]

Punishment by close confinement or reduction of diet shall never be inflicted unless the prisoner is certified by the medical officer as medically fit to sustain it.[66]

Instruments of restraint shall never be applied as a punishment.[67]

Prisoners who are subject to disciplinary action should have the right of appeal to a higher authority.[68]

VI. Making the Best Use of Prisons

The main aim of the prison authorities in their treatment of prisoners should be to encourage personal reformation and social rehabilitation.[69]

The purpose of the prison regime should be to help prisoners to lead law-abiding and self-supporting lives after their release.[70]

All sentenced prisoners who are medically fit shall be required to work. As far as possible, this work should give them skills that will enable them to earn an honest living after their release.[71]

National legislation regarding health and safety at work shall apply in prison in the same way as it does in the community.[72]

Vocational training shall be provided, especially for young prisoners.[73]

Prisoners should be remunerated for the work they do.[74]

Prisoners should be allowed to spend at least a part of their earnings, to send a part to their families and to save a part.[75]

Education and cultural activities shall be provided and encouraged, including access to an adequate library.[76]

Education in prisons should be aimed at developing the whole person, taking account of prisoners' social, economic and cultural background.[77]

Education shall be compulsory for young prisoners and illiterate prisoners. The prison authorities should give this high priority.[78]

The outside community should be involved as much as possible in educational and cultural activities in prisons.[79]

All prisoners have the right to observe the tenets of their religion and to have access to a minister of that religion.[80]

Prisoners shall be allowed access to qualified representatives of any religion.[81]

From the beginning of a prisoner's sentence consideration shall be given to his or her future after release and prisoners shall be assisted in ensuring their future reintegration into society.[82]

All agencies and services responsible for the reintegration of prisoners into society shall ensure that all prisoners have means and available resources to maintain themselves in the period immediately following their release.[83]

VII. Prisoners' Contact with the Outside World

No one shall be subjected to arbitrary interference with his or her privacy, family, home or correspondence.[84]

All prisoners shall have the right to communicate with the outside world, especially with their families.[85]

Foreign prisoners shall be allowed to communicate with their diplomatic representatives.[86]

A prisoner's request to be held in a prison near his or her home shall be granted as far as possible.[87]

Prisoners shall be kept informed of important items of news.[88]

VIII. Complaints and Inspection Procedures

Anyone whose rights and freedoms have been violated has the right to an effective remedy, determined by a competent court.[89]

Every prisoner shall have the right to make a complaint regarding his or her treatment and, unless the complaint is evidently frivolous, to have it dealt with promptly and, if requested, confidentially. If necessary, the complaint may be lodged on behalf of the prisoner by his or her legal representative or family.[90]

Every prisoner on admission shall be provided with written information on regulations and on complaints and disciplinary procedures in a language which he or she understands. If necessary, these rules should be explained orally.[91]

If a complaint is rejected or not responded to in a timely manner, the complainant shall be entitled to bring it before a judicial or other authority.[92]

States shall ensure a prompt and impartial investigation whenever there are reasonable grounds to believe that an act of torture or ill-treatment has been committed.[93]

There shall be thorough, prompt and impartial investigation of all suspected cases of extra-legal, arbitrary and summary execution, including cases where complaints by relatives or other reliable reports suggest unnatural death in the above circumstances.[94]

Prisons shall be inspected regularly by qualified and experienced inspectors from a competent authority separate from the prison administration.[95]

Every prisoner shall have the right to communicate freely and confidentially with inspectors, subject only to the demands of good order and discipline in the institution.[96]

IX. Special Categories of Prisoners

A. Non-discrimination

All persons are equal before the law and are entitled, without discrimination, to equal protection of the law.[97]

Everyone has the right to freedom of thought, conscience and religion and persons belonging to ethnic, religious or linguistic minorities have the right to their own culture, religion and language.[98]

A prisoner who does not adequately understand or speak the language used by the authorities is entitled to receive relevant information promptly in a language which he understands.[99]

Prisoners who are foreign nationals shall be allowed reasonable facilities to communicate with diplomatic representatives of their State.[100]

Prisoners who are nationals of States without diplomatic representation in the country or refugees or stateless persons shall be allowed reasonable facilities to communicate with the diplomatic representative of the State which takes charge of their interests or any national or international authority whose task it is to protect such persons.[101]

B. Women in prison

Women are entitled to the equal enjoyment and protection of all human rights in the political, economic, social, cultural, civil and all other fields.[102]

Women prisoners shall not suffer discrimination and shall be protected from all forms of violence or exploitation.[103]

Women prisoners shall be detained separately from male prisoners.[104]

Women prisoners shall be supervised and searched only by female officers and staff.[105]

Pregnant women and nursing mothers who are in prison shall be provided with the special facilities which they need for their condition.[106]

Whenever practicable, women prisoners should be taken to outside hospitals to give birth.[107]

C.   Juveniles in detention

Children are to benefit from all the human rights guarantees available to adults.[108]

In addition, the following rules shall be applied to children:

Children who are detained shall be treated in a manner which promotes their sense of dignity and worth, facilitates their reintegration into society, reflects their best interests and takes their needs into account.[109]

Children shall not be subjected to corporal punishment, capital punishment or life imprisonment without possibility of release.[110]

Children who are detained shall be separated from adult prisoners. Accused juveniles shall be separated from adults and brought for trial as speedily as possible.[111]

Special efforts shall be made to allow detained children to receive visits from and correspond with family members.[112]

The privacy of a detained child shall be respected, and complete and secure records are to be maintained and kept confidential.[113]

Juveniles of compulsory school age have the right to education and to vocational training.[114]

Weapons shall not be carried in institutions which hold juveniles.[115]

Disciplinary procedures shall respect the child's dignity and be designed to instil in the child a sense of justice, self-respect and respect for human rights.[116]

Parents are to be notified of the admission, transfer, release, sickness, injury or death of a juvenile.[117]

D. Prisoners under sentence of death

Every human being has the inherent right to life, which shall be protected by law.[118]

In countries which have not abolished the death penalty, it shall be imposed only for the most serious crimes and after a final judgement rendered by a competent court.[119]

The death penalty shall not be imposed for crimes committed by persons below the age of eighteen and shall not be carried out on pregnant women, new mothers or persons who have become insane.[120]

Where capital punishment occurs, it shall be carried out so as to inflict the minimum possible suffering.[121]

Abolition of the death penalty is encouraged.[122]

E. Life and long-term prisoners

The essential aim of the treatment of prisoners shall be their reformation and social rehabilitation.[123]

Life imprisonment without possibility of release shall not be imposed for offences committed by persons below eighteen years of age.[124]

The regime of the institution should seek to minimize any differences between prison life and life at liberty which tend to lessen the responsibility of the prisoners or the respect due to their dignity as human beings.[125]

Treatment shall be such as to encourage long-term prisoners' self-respect and to develop their sense of responsibility.[126]

Prisoners shall be allowed under necessary supervision to communicate with their family and reputable friends at regular intervals, both by correspondence and by receiving visits.[127]

Life-sentence prisoners should be eligible for release into society once they have served a sufficient period of time in custody to mark the seriousness of their offences.[128]

X. Persons under Detention without Sentence

Everyone charged with a penal offence has the right to be presumed innocent until proved guilty.[129]

Everyone has the right to liberty and security. No one shall be deprived of liberty except on such grounds and in accordance with such procedures as are established by law.[130]

Anyone who is arrested shall be informed, at the time of arrest, of the reasons for the arrest and of his or her rights. Anyone who is arrested shall be promptly informed of any charges.[131]

Anyone who is arrested shall be brought promptly before a judicial authority for the purpose of having the legality of his or her arrest or detention reviewed and shall be released if the detention is found to be unlawful.[132]

Anyone who is arrested has the right to trial within a reasonable time or to release.[133]

Comprehensive written records of all interrogations must be kept, including the identity of all persons present during the interrogation.[134]

All arrested or detained persons shall have access to a lawyer or other legal representative and adequate opportunity to communicate with that representative.[135]

Untried prisoners shall be allowed immediately to inform their families of their detention and shall be given all reasonable facilities for communicating with their families and friends.[136]

Accused persons shall, save in exceptional circumstances, be segregated from convicted persons and shall be subject to separate treatment.[137]

Untried prisoners shall sleep singly in separate rooms, with the reservation of different local custom in respect of the climate.[138]

Untried prisoners may, if they so desire, have their food procured at their own expense from the outside.[139]

Untried prisoners shall be allowed to wear their own clothing if it is clean and suitable.[140]

If an untried prisoner wears prison clothing, it shall be different from that supplied to convicted prisoners.[141]

Untried prisoners shall always be offered the opportunity to work, but shall not be required to work.[142]

Untried prisoners shall generally be allowed to procure at their own expense books, newspapers and writing materials.[143]

Untried prisoners shall generally be allowed visits from their own doctor or dentist.[144]

Persons awaiting trial shall not be detained in custody as a general rule.[145]

Release pending trial shall be envisaged as early as possible.[146]

A pre-trial prisoner shall have the right to appeal to a judicial or other independent authority against his or her detention.[147]

Persons arrested or imprisoned without charge shall be accorded the same protection and facilities as pre-trial prisoners and those awaiting trial.[148]

XI. Non-custodial Measures

The use of non-custodial measures should be recommended and encouraged.[149]

Non-custodial measures should be applied without discrimination on the grounds of race, colour, sex, age, language, religion, political or other opinion, national or social origin, property, birth or other status.[150]

Consideration should be given where possible to dealing with offenders in the community, without resort to the courts.[151]

Non-custodial measures should be used in accordance with the principle of minimum intervention.[152]

Any form of release from an institution to a non-custodial programme shall be considered at the earliest possible stage.[153]

There should be suitable mechanisms to facilitate linkages between services responsible for non-custodial measures and other relevant agencies in the criminal justice system, social development and welfare agencies, both governmental and non-governmental, in such fields as health, housing, education and labour, and the mass media.[154]

The criminal justice system should provide a wide range of non-custodial measures, from pre-trial to post-sentencing dispositions, in order to avoid the unnecessary use of imprisonment.[155]

Pre-trial detention shall be used as a means of last resort in criminal proceedings, and alternatives to pre-trial detention should be employed as early as possible.[156]

The number and types of non-custodial measures available should be determined in such a way that consistent sentencing remains possible.[157]

Sentencing authorities, when considering non-custodial measures, should take into consideration the rehabilitative needs of the offender, the protection of society and the interests of the victim, who should be consulted whenever appropriate.[158]

The development of new non-custodial measures should be encouraged and closely monitored and their use systematically evaluated.[159]

XII. The Administration of Prisons and Prison Staff

All law enforcement officials, including prison staff, shall respect and protect human dignity and maintain and uphold the human rights of all persons.[160]

The administration of the prison staff should be in civilian hands. It should not be part of a military structure.[161]

Personnel shall be carefully selected for their integrity, humanity, professional capacity and personal suitability.[162]

The prison administration should be diligent in informing the personnel and the public that prison work is a social service of great importance.[163]

Personnel shall be appointed as full-time prison officers, with civilian status, salaries adequate to attract and retain suitable men and women, and favourable employment benefits and conditions of service.[164]

Both law enforcement agencies and prison authorities shall not discriminate against women in recruitment, hiring, training, assignment, promotion, salary or other career and administrative matters.[165]

Both law enforcement agencies and prison authorities shall recruit sufficient numbers of women to ensure fair community representation and the protection of the rights of women prisoners.[166]

Personnel shall have an adequate standard of intelligence and education and shall be trained before entering on duty and while they are in service.[167]

Personnel shall conduct themselves in a manner which commands the respect of prisoners.[168]

Personnel shall include, so far as possible, sufficient numbers of specialists such as psychiatrists and psychologists, and also social workers, teachers and trade instructors.[169]

The director of an institution should be adequately qualified for his or her task, appointed on a full-time basis and resident on the premises or in the immediate vicinity.[170]

The director, his or her deputy and the majority of the other personnel shall be able to speak the language of the majority of the prisoners.[171]

There shall be adequate medical personnel resident close to the institution.[172]

In an institution for both men and women, the part of the institution set aside for women shall be under the authority of a responsible woman officer and women prisoners shall be attended and supervised only by women officers.[173]

Prison officers shall not use force, except in self-defence or in cases of attempted escape or active or passive resistance to an order based on law or regulations.[174]

Officers who have recourse to force must use only the minimum force and must report the incident immediately to the prison director.[175]

Staff in direct contact with prisoners should not usually be armed.[176]

Law enforcement officials shall respect the confidentiality of information in their possession unless the performance of duty or the needs of justice strictly require otherwise.[177]

Law enforcement officials shall ensure the full protection of the health of persons in their custody.[178]

Firearms shall not be used against persons in custody or detention except in the following circumstances:

- In self-defence or defence of others against imminent threat of death or serious injury;

- When strictly necessary to prevent the escape of a person presenting a grave threat to life.[179]

Intentional lethal use of force or firearms shall be permitted only when strictly unavoidable in order to protect human life.[180]

ENDNOTES

[1] International Covenant on Civil and Political Rights [hereinafter "ICCPR"], article 2, para. 3.

[2] Charter of the United Nations, Preamble, Article 1 and Article 55 (c).

[3] ICCPR, article 2, para. 3; Code of Conduct for Law Enforcement Officials [hereinafter "Code of Conduct"], article 2.

[4] Universal Declaration of Human Rights [hereinafter "UDHR"], preamble and article 1; ICCPR, preamble.

[5] UDHR, preamble and article 1; ICCPR, preamble.

[6] Body of Principles for the Protection of All Persons under Any Form of Detention or Imprisonment [hereinafter "Principles on Detention or Imprisonment"], principle 1; Basic Principles for the Treatment of Prisoners [hereinafter "BPT"], principle 1.

[7] UDHR, article 5; ICCPR, article 7; Convention against Torture and Other Cruel, Inhuman or Degrading Treatment or Punishment [hereinafter "CAT"], preamble and article 2; Code of Conduct, article 5.

[8] CAT, article 1.

[9] CAT, article 16.

[10] Rome Statute of the International Criminal Court, article 7.

[11] Principles on Detention or Imprisonment, principle 22.

[12] Declaration on the Protection of All Persons from Enforced Disappearance [hereinafter "Declaration on Enforced Disappearance"], article 1; Principles on the Effective Prevention and Investigation of Extra-legal, Arbitrary and Summary Executions [hereinafter "Principles on Summary Executions"], principle 1.

[13] CAT, article 10.

[14] CAT, article 15.

[15] CAT, article 2.

[16] Code of Conduct, article 3.

[17] CAT, article 13.

[18] Principles on Detention or Imprisonment, principle 34.

[19] CAT, article 11.

[20] Principles on Summary Executions, principle 6.

[21] Standard Minimum Rules for the Treatment of Prisoners [hereinafter "SMR"], rule 7; Declaration on Enforced Disappearance, article 10; Principles on Summary Executions, principle 6.

[22] Principles on Detention or Imprisonment, principle 13; SMR, rule 35.

[23] Principles on Detention or Imprisonment, principle 12; Principles on Summary Executions, principle 6.

[24] Principles on Detention or Imprisonment, principle 24; SMR, rule 24.

[25] ICCPR, article 10, para. 1.

[26] UDHR, article 25; International Covenant on Economic, Social and Cultural Rights [hereinafter "ICESCR"], article 11; Convention on the Rights of the Child [hereinafter "CRC"], article 27; Guidelines and Measures for the Prohibition and Prevention of Torture, Cruel, Inhuman or Degrading Treatment or Punishment in Africa [hereinafter "Robben Island Guidelines"], paragraph 34.

[27] SMR, rule 10.

[28] SMR, rule 9 (2).

[29] ICESCR, article 11.

[30] SMR, rule 20.

[31] ICESCR, article 11.

[32] SMR, rule 17 (1).

[33] SMR, rules 17 (2) and 18.

[34] SMR, rule 19.

[35] SMR, rule 19.

[36] ICESCR, article 12.

[37] Principles on Detention or Imprisonment, principle 24; SMR, rule 24.

[38] Principles on Detention or Imprisonment, principle 24.

[39] Principles on Detention or Imprisonment, principle 25.

[40] UDHR, article 25; ICESCR, article 12.

[41] BPT, principle 9.

[42] SMR, rule 25.

[43] SMR, rule 26.

[44] SMR, rule 22 (1) and (2).

[45] SMR, rule 22 (3).

[46] SMR, rule 22 (1).

[47] SMR, rule 82 (1).

[48] SMR, rule 82 (2).

[49] SMR, rule 82 (3).

[50] SMR, rule 22 (1).

[51] Principles of Medical Ethics relevant to the Role of Health Personnel, particularly Physicians, in the Protection of Prisoners and Detainees against Torture and Other Cruel, Inhuman or Degrading Treatment or Punishment [hereinafter "Principles of Medical Ethics"], principle 1.

[52] Principles of Medical Ethics, principles 1 to 6.

[53] Principles of Medical Ethics, principles 1 to 6.

[54] SMR, rules 12 to 16.

[55] SMR, rule 21.

[56] Basic Principles on the Use of Force and Firearms by Law Enforcement Officials [hereinafter "Principles on Force and Firearms"], principle 9.

[57] SMR, rule 33.

[58] SMR, rule 27.

[59] SMR, rule 27.

[60] SMR, rule 33.

[61] SMR, rule 27.

[62] Principles on Detention or Imprisonment, principle 30; SMR, rules 29 and 30.

[63] SMR, rule 30 (2).

[64] SMR, rule 28 (1).

[65] SMR, rule 31.

[66] SMR, rule 32.

[67] SMR, rule 33.

[68] ICCPR, article 2; Principles on Detention or Imprisonment, principle 30, para. 2.

[69] ICCPR, article 10, para. 3.

[70] SMR, rules 65 and 66 (1).

[71] SMR, rules 66 (1) and 71; BPT, principle 8.

[72] SMR, rules 72 (1) and 74.

[73] SMR, rule 71 (5).

[74] UDHR, article 23; SMR, rule 76 (1).

[75] SMR, rule 76 (2) and (3).

[76] UDHR, articles 26 and 27; ICESCR, article 13; SMR, rules 40, 77 and 78.

[77] BPT, principle 6; Economic and Social Council resolution 1990/20 of 24 May 1990, paragraph 3 (a).

[78] SMR, rule 77.

[79] Economic and Social Council resolution 1990/20 of 24 May 1990, paragraph 3 (i).

[80] UDHR, article 18; ICCPR, article 18.

[81] SMR, rule 41.

[82] SMR, rule 80.

[83] SMR, rule 81; BPT, principle 10.

[84] UDHR, article 12; ICCPR, article 17.

[85] Principles on Detention or Imprisonment, principle 19; SMR, rules 37 and 79.

[86] SMR, rule 38.

[87] Principles on Detention or Imprisonment, principle 20.

[88] SMR, rule 39.

[89] ICCPR, article 2; CAT, article 13; Principles on Detention or Imprisonment, principle 33.

[90] Principles on Detention or Imprisonment, principle 33; SMR, rule 36.

[91] SMR, rule 35.

[92] Principles on Detention or Imprisonment, principle 33, para. 4.

[93] CAT, article 12; Principles on the Effective Investigation and Documentation of Torture and Other Cruel, Inhuman or Degrading Treatment or Punishment, principle 2.

[94] Principles on Summary Executions, principle 9.

[95] Principles on Detention or Imprisonment, principle 29, para. 1; SMR, rule 55.

[96] SMR, rules 36 (2) and 55; Principles on Detention or Imprisonment, principle 29, para. 2.

[97] UDHR, article 7; ICCPR, articles 2 and 26; International Convention on the Elimination of All Forms of Racial Discrimination, articles 2 and 5.

[98] UDHR, article 18; ICCPR, articles 18 and 27.

[99] Principles on Detention or Imprisonment, principle 14.

[100] SMR, rule 38 (1).

[101] SMR, rule 38 (2).

[102] UDHR, article 2; ICCPR, article 3; Convention on the Elimination of All Forms of Discrimination against Women [hereinafter "CEDAW"], articles 1, 2 and 3; Declaration on the Elimination of Violence against Women [hereinafter "Declaration on Violence against Women"], article 3.

[103] CEDAW, articles 1, 6 and 7; Declaration on Violence against Women, articles 2 and 4.

[104] Principles on Detention or Imprisonment, principle 5; SMR, rule 8 (a).

[105] SMR, rule 53.

[106] SMR, rule 23 (1).

[107] SMR, rule 23 (1).

[108] UDHR, article 1 and article 25, para. 2; CRC, preamble; ICCPR, preamble.

[109] CRC, articles 3 and 37; United Nations Standard Minimum Rules for the Administration of Juvenile Justice (The Beijing Rules) [hereinafter "Beijing Rules"], rules 1, 5 and 6; United Nations Rules for the Protection of Juveniles Deprived of their Liberty [hereinafter "Rules for Juveniles"], rules 1, 4, 14, 31, 79 and 80.

[110] CRC, article 37 (a); Beijing Rules, rule 27; Rules for Juveniles, rules 64, 66 and 67.

[111] ICCPR, article 10, para. 2 (b); CRC, article 37 (c); Beijing Rules, rules 13.4 and 26.3; Rules for Juveniles, rule 29.

[112] CRC, articles 9, 10 and 37 (c); Beijing Rules, rules 13.3, 26.5 and 27.2; SMR, rule 37; Rules for Juveniles, rule 59.

[113] CRC, article 40, para. 2 (b) (vii); Beijing Rules, rule 21.1.

[114] ICESCR, article 13; CRC, article 28; Rules for Juveniles, rules 38 and 42.

[115] Rules for Juveniles, rule 65.

[116] Rules for Juveniles, rule 66.

117 CRC, article 37 (c) and article 40, para. 2 (b) (ii); Beijing Rules, rules 10.1 and 26.5; SMR, rules 37 and 44; Rules for Juveniles, rules 56 and 57.

118 UDHR, article 3; ICCPR, article 6, para. 1.

119 ICCPR, article 6, para. 2; Safeguards guaranteeing protection of the rights of those facing the death penalty [hereinafter "Death Penalty Safeguards"], para. 1.

120 ICCPR, article 6, para. 5; Death Penalty Safeguards, para. 3.

121 Death Penalty Safeguards, para. 9.

122 ICCPR, article 6, para. 6.

123 ICCPR, article 10, para. 3.

124 CRC, article 37 (a).

125 SMR, rule 60 (1).

126 SMR, rules 65 and 66.

127 SMR, rule 37.

128 Resolution (76) 2 of 17 February 1976 of the Committee of Ministers of the Council of Europe on the treatment of long-term prisoners.

129 UDHR, article 11; ICCPR, article 14, para. 2; Principles on Detention or Imprisonment, principle 36; SMR, rule 84 (2).

130 UDHR, article 3; ICCPR, article 9, para. 1.

131 ICCPR, article 9, para. 2, and article 14, para. 3 (a); Principles on Detention or Imprisonment, principle 10.

132 ICCPR, article 9, para. 4; Principles on Detention or Imprisonment, principle 37.

133 ICCPR, article 9, para. 3; Principles on Detention or Imprisonment, principle 38.

134 Robben Island Guidelines, para. 28.

135 UDHR, article 11; ICCPR, article 14, para. 3 (b) and (d); Principles on Detention or Imprisonment, principles 17 and 18; SMR, rule 93.

136 Principles on Detention or Imprisonment, principle 16, para. 1; SMR, rules 44 (3) and 92; Declaration on Enforced Disappearance, article 10, para. 2; Principles on Summary Executions, principle 6.

137 ICCPR, article 10, para. 2 (a); Principles on Detention or Imprisonment, principle 8; SMR, rules 8 (b) and 85 (1).

[138] SMR, rule 86.
[139] SMR, rule 87.
[140] SMR, rule 88 (1).
[141] SMR, rule 88 (2).
[142] SMR, rule 89.
[143] SMR, rule 90; Principles on Detention or Imprisonment, principle 28.
[144] SMR, rule 91.
[145] ICCPR, article 9, para. 3.
[146] Principles on Detention or Imprisonment, principle 39; United Nations Standard Minimum Rules for Non-custodial Measures (The Tokyo Rules) [hereinafter "Tokyo Rules"], rule 6.2.
[147] Tokyo Rules, rule 6.3.
[148] SMR, rule 95.
[149] Tokyo Rules, rule 1.
[150] Tokyo Rules, rule 2.2.
[151] Tokyo Rules, rule 2.5.
[152] Tokyo Rules, rule 2.6.
[153] Tokyo Rules, rule 9.4.
[154] Tokyo Rules, rule 22.
[155] Tokyo Rules, rule 2.3.
[156] ICCPR, article 9, para. 3; Tokyo Rules, rules 5 and 6.
[157] Tokyo Rules, rules 2.3 and 8.1.
[158] Tokyo Rules, rule 8.1.
[159] Tokyo Rules, rule 2.4.
[160] ICCPR, preamble; Code of Conduct, article 2.
[161] SMR, rule 46 (3).
[162] SMR, rule 46 (1).
[163] SMR, rule 46 (2).
[164] SMR, rule 46 (3).
[165] UDHR, article 2; ICCPR, articles 2, 3 and 26; CEDAW, preamble and articles 2, 3 and 7 (*b*); General Assembly resolution 34/169 of 17 December 1979 (resolution adopting the Code of Conduct for Law Enforcement Officials), eighth preambular paragraph, subpara. (*a*).

[166] General Assembly resolution 34/169 of 17 December 1979, eighth preambular paragraph, subpara. (*a*); SMR, rule 53.

[167] SMR, rule 47.

[168] SMR, rule 48; Code of Conduct, article 8.

[169] SMR, rule 49.

[170] SMR, rule 50.

[171] SMR, rule 51 (1).

[172] SMR, rule 52.

[173] SMR, rule 53.

[174] SMR, rule 54 (1); Code of Conduct, article 3; Principles on Force and Firearms, principles 4 and 15.

[175] Principles on Force and Firearms, principle 5.

[176] SMR, rule 54 (3).

[177] Code of Conduct, article 4.

[178] Code of Conduct, article 6.

[179] Principles on Force and Firearms, principle 9.

[180] Principles on Force and Firearms, principle 9.